Dump Trucks

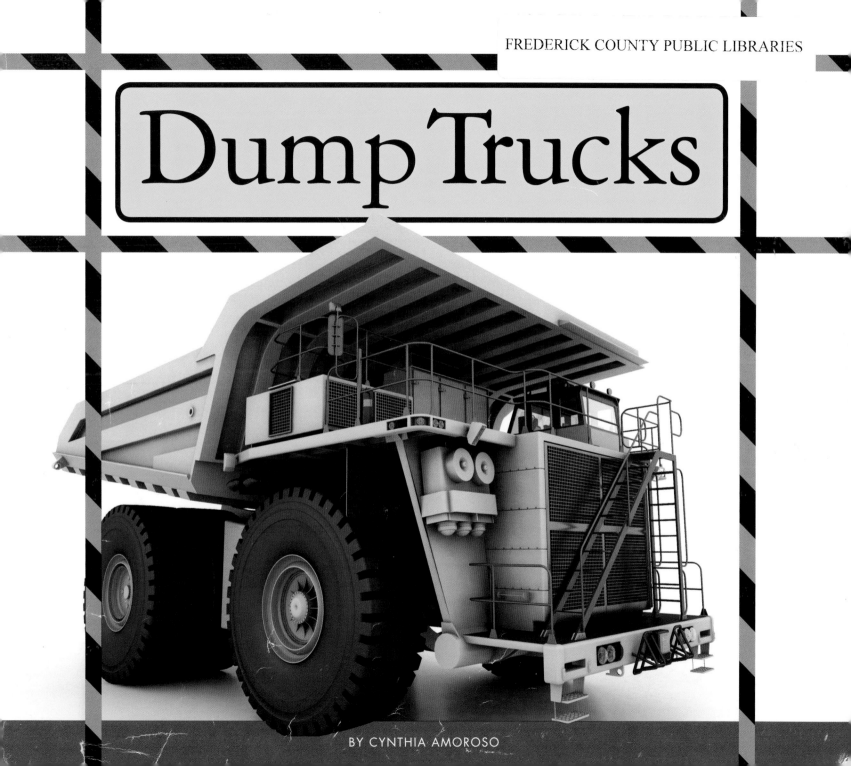

BY CYNTHIA AMOROSO

The
Child's
World®

Published by The Child's World®
1980 Lookout Drive • Mankato, MN 56003-1705
800-599-READ • www.childsworld.com

Acknowledgments
The Child's World®: Mary Berendes, Publishing Director
The Design Lab: Design
Jody Jensen Shaffer; Editing
Pamela J. Mitsakos: Photo Research

Photos
abutyrin/Shutterstock.com: 7; Andrey N Bannov/
Shutterstock: 12, 20; Bonita R. Cheshier/Shutterstock.
com: 8; David M. Budd Photography: 19; dragunov/
Shutterstock.com: 4; Eric Milos/Shutterstock.com:
cover, 1; Faraways/Shutterstock.com: 15; johnnorth/
iStock.com: 16; risteski goce/Shutterstock.com: 11

ISBN 9781623239671
LCCN 2013947253

Printed in the United States of America
Mankato, MN
July, 2014
PA02237

Contents

This dump truck is leaving a *quarry*. It is carrying rocks.

What are dump trucks?

Dump trucks are special kinds of **vehicles**. They carry loose things such as dirt, rocks, and sand. Then they tip them out. Most dump trucks are large. They can carry heavy loads.

How are dump trucks used?

Dump trucks are often used when people build things. Sometimes they carry **gravel** for building roads. Sometimes they bring dirt to fill in low places. Sometimes they carry away extra dirt or rocks.

These dump trucks are on their way to be filled with gravel.

7

This driver runs the whole truck from the cab. He drives the truck from place to place. He works the dumper body, too.

What are the parts of a dump truck?

The front of the dump truck has a **cab**. The driver sits in the cab. The back of the truck has a dumper body. It holds the dirt or rocks.

How does a dump truck move?

A dump truck is a lot like other trucks. It has an **engine** that makes it move. The engine runs on **diesel fuel**. The engine makes power that turns the truck's wheels. The driver moves the truck from place to place.

A dump truck's engine is in the front.

11

A special machine loads this dump truck. It empties a big scoop into the dumper body.

12

How do you load a dump truck?

A dump truck cannot load itself. Other machines fill the dumper body. They lift the dirt above the dumper body. Then they drop it in.

How does a dump truck dump?

Dump trucks unload themselves! Many of them work fairly simply. The worker uses the truck's **controls** to dump the load. A special part lifts the front of the dumper body. The dirt or rocks slide out the back.

All of the rocks have slid from the back of this dump truck.

15

This dump truck is unloading huge rocks at a quarry.

How much can a dump truck carry?

Dump trucks are made to carry big, heavy loads. The biggest can carry 20,000 pounds (9,072 kg). That is as much as 13 cows!

Are there different kinds of dump trucks?

There are many kinds of dump trucks. They come in different sizes and shapes. They have different kinds of dumper bodies. They have different ways of getting rid of their loads.

This truck's dumper body tips sideways. The load lands in a long pile.

19

Watching a dump truck unload can be fun.

Are dump trucks useful?

Dump trucks are very useful. They do lots of hard, dirty work. They are great for carrying rocks and other heavy loads. And they are very easy to unload. They are also fun to watch!

GLOSSARY

cab (KAB) A machine's cab is the area where the driver sits.

controls (kun-TROHLZ) Controls are parts that people use to run a machine.

diesel fuel (DEE-sul FYOOL) Diesel fuel is a heavy oil that is burned to make power.

engine (EN-jun) An engine is a machine that makes something move.

gravel (GRAV-ull) Gravel is loose, small stones.

quarry (KWOR-ree) A quarry is a place where stone is dug up from the ground.

vehicles (VEE-uh-kullz) Vehicles are things for carrying people or goods.

BOOKS

Jango-Cohen, Judith. *Dump Trucks*. Minneapolis, MN: Lerner, 2003.

Kawa, Katie. *Dump Trucks*. New York: Gareth Stevens, 2012.

Teitelbaum, Michael, and Uldis Klavins (illustrator). *If I Could Drive a Dump Truck!* New York: Scholastic, 2001.

WEB SITES

Visit our Web site for lots of links about dump trucks:
childsworld.com/links

Note to parents, teachers, and librarians: We routinely check our Web links to make sure they're safe, active sites—so encourage your readers to check them out!

INDEX

ABOUT THE AUTHOR

Even as a child, Cynthia Amoroso knew she wanted to be a writer. She is always working to involve kids in reading and writing, and she loves spending time in the children's section of the library or bookstore. Cynthia enjoys gardening, traveling, and having fun with friends and family.